So Happy
TOGETHER

120 Creative Ways To Strengthen Your Marriage

HONOR **HB** BOOKS

Inspiration and Motivation for the Seasons of Life

COOK COMMUNICATIONS MINISTRIES
Colorado Springs, Colorado • Paris, Ontario
KINGSWAY COMMUNICATIONS LTD
Eastbourne, England

Honor® is an imprint of
Cook Communications Ministries, Colorado Springs, CO 80918
Cook Communications, Paris, Ontario
Kingsway Communications, Eastbourne, England

SO HAPPY TOGETHER: 120 CREATIVE WAYS TO STRENGTHEN YOUR MARRIAGE
© 2006 by Honor Books

Compiled by Kerry Park

Cover and Interior Design: BMB Design

First Printing, 2006
Printed in the United States of America

1 2 3 4 5 6 7 8 9 10 Printing/Year 10 09 08 07 06

Scripture quotations are taken from the HOLY BIBLE, NEW INTERNATIONAL VERSION®.
Copyright © 1973, 1978, 1984 International Bible Society. Used by permission of
Zondervan. All rights reserved.

ISBN 1-56292-755-8

Introduction

So Happy Together doesn't have to describe how your marriage used to be—it can be the way you feel forever.

Let's face it, couples can fall into a rut where their highest hope is just to survive their marriage. If this is where you are in your marriage, it's time to reevaluate and start working toward being *So Happy Together*. This book reveals twelve essential commitment areas that can change how you do marriage—starting today! Learn to leave behind past failures, disappointments, and ineffective patterns. *So Happy Together* will show you how hope can be renewed and the sweet joy of first love restored.

All it takes is a little work and you and your spouse will be on your way to being *So Happy Together*.

What would you give for one, really good year of marriage?
How about one great year that becomes
the foundation for endless others?
This little book will give you the foundation to live
So Happy Together *forever!*

So maybe right now you're just surviving marriage.
You've probably experienced:

- *Moments of agony*
- *Unrealistic expectations*
- *Tearful tragedies*
- *Communication gridlock*

- *Moments of ecstasy*
- *Astounding surprises*
- *Accepted apologies*
- *Moments of connection*

Let's look at how you would describe where you are in your marriage.

Are you happily connected or hopelessly disconnected?

Have children brought you closer to each other, or left you distant from each other?

Has your marriage turned into a business partnership dedicated to raising great kids, or have you maintained a thriving "us" over the years?

How do you react to the words "starting over"?
Does it leave you pessimistic?

Do you tell yourself …
Why bother, we've tried so many times before?

Sometimes "starting over" means we white wash our problems, close our eyes, avoid, ignore, and deny the challenges before us.

But denial is about as useful as rearranging the deck chairs on the *Titanic*.

But you can change your unproductive patterns of interacting. You can stop repeating the same mistakes.

A lobster has to regularly shed its shell when it feels cramped. In that same way, we need to admit that we continually need to revitalize our marriage.

Regardless of the years you have invested in your marriage, regardless of the mistakes and the pain, it's time to shed that hard shell and risk vulnerability so that you can become happy together again!

It's time to dare to believe that you can grow into a new level of relationship that fits both of you better than anything you have ever encountered.

If you are willing to take the risk and work at creating one good year of marriage, you can create positive patterns and repeat them each successive year.

No matter what your marriage has been like, you can be happy together—now and forever!

You need to know that relationship problems aren't solved by ending relationships.

Rather than entertaining the idea of divorcing your partner,
you need to divorce the way you do marriage!

If you've been married for a number of years, you understand the inclination to let old habits hang on. After all, they are familiar. On one hand they are comfortable, but on the other hand, they are so unfulfilling.

If **you want to spend the rest of your marriage being happy together, challenge yourself to a new way of doing marriage.**

Remain committed to the marriage, to valuing each other, to expressing your love and respect while changing habits that thwart your goals.

What your marriage was, it was.
Now it's time to create what it can be.

Everyone loves to be in the presence of an encourager. Encouragers energize us. They think the best of us. They attribute the best intentions to our words and actions, and challenge us to be all that we can be.

An encouraging spirit provides a welcome retreat for any of us with battle scars from dealing with the world at large.

On the other hand, a critical spirit makes a marriage brittle. Criticism cuts to the core, and as a result, love becomes fragile and weak rather than strong and robust as it should be.

A husband or wife is in a unique position to give their partner something hard to find anywhere else—encouragement.

Being an encourager to our partner is a priceless gift.

Encouragement: *Taking Stock*

Check any of the following statements that are true of you.

_____ I find it hard to accept my partner's differences.

_____ I feel critical at least three times a week.

_____ I use my mouth as a weapon when I'm upset, making my partner feel small.

_____ When I'm upset, I point out my partner's dysfunction.

_____ When I'm upset, I disengage from the conversation.

_____ When I'm upset, I threaten to leave.

_____ When I'm upset, I consistently use the word "you" followed by a critical put-down.

_____ When I'm upset, I wait for my partner to apologize; I rarely make an attempt to repair the relationship.

What did you learn about yourself from these questions?

If you checked the majority of these statements, you need to think carefully about your own attitudes rather than your partner's shortcomings.

All **married people get angry and frustrated with their partner.**

Frustrations and irritations don't kill love. But the consistent habit of making your partner feel small, minimized, and demeaned will surely kill it.

Remember, marriage is NOT a reform school.
The only person you can change is yourself, and that is work enough.

Whoever would love life and see good days must keep his tongue from evil and his lips from deceitful speech. He must turn from evil and do good; he must seek peace and pursue it. For the eyes of the Lord are on the righteous and his ears are attentive to their prayer, but the face of the Lord is against those who do evil.

1 Peter 3:10-12

Heart 2 Heart

How would you complete this statement?

The thing I enjoy most about my partner is_____.

What specific areas of your partner's life could you pray
that the Lord will bless?

A Prayer for Encouragement
Lord, allow me to see my partner through your eyes.
Help me to be the encourager my partner needs me to be.
And help my partner be the encourager I need.

I commit on a daily basis to be an encouraging partner.

My Second Commitment:

Intentional Choices

Commit to make intentional choices that enrich your marriage.

When we commit ourselves to intentional choice, we leave behind complacency.

Why should we choose what is best for our partner
when he or she doesn't deserve it?
Because this is the kind of person we want to be.
Values motivate us to give more of
ourselves than seems "fair."

When we make intentional choices, we are choosing to live out of our value system. We cannot be true to ourselves without being true to our values.

Intentionality in attitude and action can transform a relationship.

Dependency gets in the way of love.

Being unable or unwilling to act independently, a dependent person relies heavily on their spouse.

By contrast, an intentional partner is aware of how important personal choices are to the domestic, romantic, financial, spiritual, social, and intimate aspects of marriage.

An intentional partner initiates loving actions even when the feelings of love are temporarily blocked.

When both partners intentionally use their freedom to give, to serve, and to love the other, their relationship is rejuvenated.

In 1 Corinthians 13:5 the apostle Paul writes that love is not self-seeking.

An intentional marriage supports the process of each other's growth.

YOU AND YOUR VALUES: *Taking Stock*

Circle five values and ideals that you would
want someone to use to describe you.

Love	Charity	Kindness
Joy	Courage	Generosity
Peace	Tolerance	Competence
Patience	Stability	Moderation
Goodness	Flexibility	Hope
Self-control	Attentiveness	Integrity
Availability	Compassion	Personal strength
Service	Creativity	Mercy
Understanding	Hospitality	Trust
Faith	Gentleness	Empathy
Wisdom	Faithfulness	Optimism
Humor	Equality	Other _____

Heart 2 Heart

Share your answers to this personal inventory with your partner.

Ask your partner if there are specific ways that you can encourage him or her to live according to his or her five values.

Combine your two lists of top five values. Is there any overlap? These mutually shared values can help guide your life as a couple.

Did either of you learn something new about your partner when you looked at each other's values?

So, it's true. Every marriage can catch a case of the blahs. Maybe nothing terrible is wrong, but nothing is particularly right either. You're simply too busy, too tired, or too stressed to relate effectively.

But think about this:
Five minutes devoted to romance equals one day of harmony!

Intentional choices are incredibly powerful.

Here Are Some Practical Ways to Make Intentional Choices.

- Express your love to your partner in words today.

- Check in with your partner at least one time during the day.

- Be affectionate with your partner today (hold hands, give hugs, cuddle without pushing for anything else).

- Kiss your partner good-bye and hello.

- Lighten your partner's load in one specific way, without being asked.

Take Steps to Help You Live "On Purpose."

Pick an evening, sit down with a master calendar for the week, and create intentional times of connection, such as:

A date time once a week

A time of daily connection (a cup of coffee, discuss the interesting things going on in your day, listen to music, turn off the TV)

A time for sexual intimacy

Weekly issue discussion time to work on tough issues

Heart 2 Heart

Write out a prayer thanking God for your partner.

Ask Jesus to grow your partner into the person he or she wants to be.

Read the prayer you have written to your partner. Exchange prayers.
Put the prayer in a place where you can read it once a day
all month long.

I commit to make intentional choices that enrich our marriage.

My Third Commitment:

Forgiveness

Commit to forgive and to be aware of your need for forgiveness.

When we commit ourselves to forgive, we leave behind toxic hurts.

Every marriage experiences tension, conflict, hurt, pain and injury, misunderstanding, suffering, and alienation. This is reality. That's why forgiveness is essential.

You've heard the line, "Love means never having to say you are sorry."

NOT TRUE.

It is human to make a mistake.

But there is something wrong if we can't admit it.

Forgiveness is not a one-time event in marriage. It is a process of increasing compassion and reducing resentment as we continue to forgive. Forgiveness draws us toward each other again.

Forgiveness frees us to face our tomorrows, confident that we're not carrying past baggage, thereby halting the cycle of blame and pain.

YOUR APPROACH TO HURT AND FORGIVENESS:
Taking Stock

When you are hurt, do you …

____ Pretend that you weren't hurt?

____ Excuse or condone your partner? "It really wasn't his or her fault."

____ Deny your partner's responsibility? "He or she didn't mean to do it."

____ Give permission to continue the behavior? "Men will be men."

Where did you get your model of forgiveness?
Explain what happened to your spirit as a result of acting on one of the approaches above. How did it impact your partner?

There is a difference between false and true forgiveness.

Forgiveness is truly complete when …

You've listened completely and can see the situation through your partner's eyes.

You have addressed what you need in order to heal.

Your approach to problems is solution-oriented, not blame-oriented.

You have committed never to use the event as Exhibit A in an angry interchange.

Conflicts are worked through. They do not escalate.

You can verbalize the learning that has taken place.

When we hurt someone, our response is all-important.

Godly sorrow leads to repentance.

Rather than being self-focused, godly sorrow's focus is on the person we have just hurt and our damaged relationship.

Godly sorrow abandons guilt and moves toward the restoration of the relationship.

As the recipient of God's amazing love, we are to pass on that same love to others.

Heart *2* Heart

I live **with** you—I love you and level with you.

I care for you and I confront you.

I speak my truth as I offer you grace.

I commit to forgive and to be aware of my need for forgiveness!

My Fourth Commitment:

Awareness

Commit to awareness of your partner in your marriage.

When we commit ourselves to awareness, we leave behind apathy.

Couples dating before marriage talk nonstop.
They look into each other's eyes.
They touch.
They ask questions.
They assume there is more to know.
They are aware!

After being married for years, partners have a tendency to carve out their individual worlds.

We need to maintain awareness of our loved one. When we are truly aware, we acknowledge that our partner is a separate, fascinating human being.

There is always more to discover about each other, always more to learn.

Awareness assumes growth.

Awareness energizes.

Awareness gets specific.

Awareness praises.

Awareness initiates.

Awareness rejuvenates.

Awareness turns lifetime lovers into friends.

Awareness needs to be cultivated in a healthy marriage.

Heart 2 Heart

Share an example from your marriage when you realized that you had put your relationship on automatic pilot.

Perhaps you stopped talking or took each other for granted.

How does your current relationship compare to when you were dating? What was it like to be together?

What did you value and appreciate about each other?

Over the coming months, take a couple of these questions with you one date night or share your response over a cup of coffee. Become more aware!

What book has had the most effect on you? In what way did it impact you?

If you could live anywhere in the world for one year and not have to work, where you want to go? Why?

What was your favorite subject in school?

Do you use that subject in your job today?

What is your favorite holiday? What do you most like about it?

What is one thing in life you haven't done that you regret not doing?

If you had to spend three months alone on an island, what possessions, beside those essential for survival, would you want to have with you? Why?

If you were casting a film about your life, who would play the main characters?

What's the best advice anyone has ever given you?

Would you rather be married to a famous person, or be famous yourself?

What is the best compliment you could ever receive about your work?

Discover what's important to your partner.

If you and your partner were forced to flee your home with only three items each, what would they be?

Why did your partner choose this object, and why do you think it is important to your partner?

What does this object say about your partner?

How do you each feel about the way your partner sees you as suggested by the selection of your prized possessions?

Resist apathy in your relationship and take note of some of the following attributes of your partner:

A favorite expression he or she uses.

A tender moment that your partner shared with one of your children.

Some emotion that you thought you saw in your partner's eyes.

A moment of shared empathy that felt wonderful.

An outfit that made your partner look extra attractive to you.

A physical feature of your partner that you enjoy.

Don't you become happier just focusing on your loved one?

Continue to practice the art of awareness regarding your partner. Look at your partner through the eyes of an artist. Each day share two new observations with him or her about how he or she relates to you and others, something you value about who your partner is.

To know someone *is* to love someone.

I commit to practice awareness of my partner on an ongoing basis.

My Fifth Commitment:

Boundaries

Commit to boundaries in your marriage.

When we commit ourselves to boundaries, we
leave behind indifference.

Partners make their relationship a priority by constructing a protective wall around it, but they also make sure there are no walls between the two of them.

Boundaries in marriage are fundamental to love.

We prove that we are not indifferent to what goes on around us and choose to make our marriage a priority.

An important task in marriage is learning when to say *yes* and when to say *no*. We need to ask ourselves the following question:
If I say yes to this request, will it strengthen our marriage, and will I stay true to my value system?

A wise woman who was gaining a daughter-in-law told her son that wives always come before mothers. It's no surprise her daughter-in-law and she became good friends.

In every choice a couple makes, they need to consider their marriage. Partners need to consider each other in everything they do—especially in the touchy area of dealing with in-laws.

Interestingly, the theme of leaving parents to be joined to a partner is repeated five times in Scripture. It must have been important, don't you think?

Incredible pain results when one partner continues to allow or foster parental intrusion in the marriage.

Which of the following challenges have you and your partner faced with parents and parents-in-law?

They visit too often.

They stay too long.

They phone too little or too often.

They come over, and they take over.

They expect to be waited on and rarely lift a finger.

They fail to keep confidences.

They are critical of my partner.

They embroil us in their problems.

At different stages in marriage, it's good to reevaluate your boundary setting with parents.

Setting Boundaries with Our Children

Sometimes we can be so focused on our children that we lose
sight of our marriage.

Has having children had any kind of negative effects on your marriage?
Discuss.

Do your children honor your privacy? Would you like to make changes so
that they would? What kind of changes could you make?

Other Boundaries That Can Benefit the Marriage Relationship:

Work boundaries

Friend boundaries

Boundaries with the opposite sex

Boundaries with an ex-spouse

Boundaries with ministry and community involvement

Boundaries with addictions

Boundaries with hobbies, sports, TV, and computers

Heart 2 Heart

In the last month, what intruders have you had to limit in order to protect the boundary around your relationship?

How have you accomplished this?

What effect has this had on your relationship?

Make sure you and your partner are in agreement on the need for privacy.

Search for and discover ways to work together to regain and maintain your private time.

I commit to protect the boundaries of our marriage.

My Sixth Commitment:

Connecting

Commit to connecting in your marriage.

When we commit ourselves to connecting, we
leave behind distance.

People who are "connectors" delight in the question, *Who is this fascinating person I married?*

Connectors expect two opinions, tastes, and needs to be brought to the marriage.

Connectors embrace their partner's differences
with respect and curiosity because learning often
comes as a result of differences.

Love grows out of differences, not sameness.

Connectors build a reservoir of goodwill through small tasks that are done together, quiet conversations when the day's pressures are set aside, soft words of understanding, encouragement offered in difficult moments, and the small unexpected gift that says, *I thought of you today.*

As wonderful as being connected sounds, our human nature often takes us in another direction. Which of these common ways to avoid connecting do you use?

___ I sometimes …

___ Withdrawal into silence

___ Minimize how I feel

___ Fudge about how I am really doing

___ Keep much too active or busy

___ Value performance over relationship

Continued

___ Project my needs onto others

___ Avoid connection because of past hurts

___ See my partner as someone hurtful from my past

___ View myself as unlovable

___ Become aggressive and argumentative when I get close to my partner

___ Devalue my partner's feelings, actions, and love

___ Become an independent, "anti-need" hot-shot

___ Spiritualize pain

Marriage is a paradox: We are one, yet it takes two distinct and different partners to create an "us."

Boundary lovers in marriage are unique.
They expect, anticipate, and learn from their partner's differences.
They understand that their partner's "otherness" is fundamentally what makes love possible. They dare to explore their differences.
They can agree to disagree.

If we understand boundaries, we don't have to keep establishing distance in order to feel safe. No one has to be afraid of being swallowed up by the other.

Ask God to transform you from a detacher to a connector.

I commit to connect in healthy ways on a daily basis.

My Seventh Commitment:

Laughter

Commit to laughing in your marriage.

When we commit ourselves to laughing, we leave
behind intensity.

She wanted a husband and put an advertisement in the personal column. She got two hundred replies, all saying, "You can have mine!"

Laughter **lowers our stress. It's like oil in a car. Without it, all we get is friction and sparks.**

Laughter can change our moods, raise our spirits, quell our fears, and stop our tears.

Laughter revolutionizes our perspectives.

Laughter and humor can keep things in perspective and renew your love relationship.

Laughter is a gift, but it is also a choice, a discipline, and an art.

Healthy laughter draws us closer to each other.

The couple who laughs together feels connected to one another in the midst of life's curve balls and painful realities.

The shortest distance between two partners is a smile.

Has your marriage been enhanced and
renewed by laughter?

Be a creative initiator of fun!

What would your partner say are three things about
you that demonstrate you love life?

$\mathcal{D}o$ something to inject playfulness and laughter
into your sex life.

We can sometimes forget sex is supposed to be fun.
Laughter shared by lovers is a powerful aphrodisiac.
It defuses nervousness and inhibition.

Heart 2 Heart

Create a list of people who make you and your partner laugh. Create a list of movies that make you both laugh.

How do you feel about surprises?

How might you enjoy being surprised by your partner?

How might you best surprise him or her?

I commit to making joy and laughter part of our relationship.

My Eighth Commitment:

Teamwork

Commit to teamwork in your marriage.

When we commit ourselves to teamwork, we
leave behind the power struggle.

Just about everything we accomplish in life
depends on teamwork.

Teamwork involves …
Pulling together. Planning together. Praying together. Proceeding together.

Teamwork involves …
Shared values, vision, and mutually beneficial goals.

Teamwork embraces …
Each other's perspectives and maximizes each other's strengths.

What kind of a team have you created in the recent years of your marriage? Hierarchical? Competitive? A partnership?

Is your team big enough for two?

How open are you to your partner's perspective?

What one thing could you do that would move you in the direction of a healthy partnership?

The "Power Struggle"

Teamwork can be derailed by power struggles.

Even when you love someone, you may sometimes find it hard to live with him or her because you're so different.

Welcome to marriage!

See if you can relate to these examples:

I'm a morning person, but my partner's a night person. On the weekend half the day is shot before we can do anything.
I want to save as much money as possible for retirement; my partner is a spender.
He wants to downsize, while I want to buy a bigger house.

Power **struggles happen when issues become a "my way" versus "your way" dilemma.**

Power struggles can be a pivotal point in a marriage. How we handle the struggle determines whether we will be a team player or an adversary.

Which of these ten obstacles to teamwork have you encountered recently?

1. The misunderstanding of what is yours to control, and the belief that you have the power and the right to change the actions or the attitudes of your partner.

2. The belief that the area of decision making is your only opportunity to assert individuality in your marriage.

3. The misunderstanding of the difference between influence and control.

4. The belief that if you are open to and go along with your partner's suggestion, you are being controlled.

5. The refusal to move out of your comfort zone.

Continued

6. The placement of too much emphasis on conflicting values and vision.

7. The rigidity, inflexibility, and selfishness that says if marriage is all about "you" there can be no "us."

8. The failure to take responsibility by not following through on promises or commitments, causing the team to suffer.

9. The habit of bringing in another person to support your perspective.

10. The inability to admit your own needs and limitations.

How we handle each other's mistakes is a make-it-or-break-it issue for teamwork.

If we attack each other for making a mistake, our team is annihilated.

Teamwork is our best hope for staying strong together.

I commit to teamwork in our marriage.

My Ninth Commitment:

Faith

Commit to faith as the foundation of your marriage.

When we commit ourselves to faith, we leave behind religion.

When both partners are dedicated to becoming the man or woman God wants them to be, God becomes the One who is ultimately in charge of the marriage.

Each partner will change because God desires it, not because his or her partner deserves it.

As we let God have more of us, he is ready to give us more of himself. Our partners can't help but benefit from God's place in our lives.

A growing mutual faith solidifies our marriage.

We each experience a deeper more intimate understanding of what is on each other's heart. We have fewer masks that we hide behind, and as a result, we are more relaxed and a more connected.

Growing Spiritually as Partners Does Not Mean . . .

We will never argue, struggle, disagree, disappoint, or lose it with each other.

We will be immune from trouble, from an affair, or from divorce.

We will feel connected and in love all the time.

We will always see eye to eye.

We will no longer be irked by each other's differences.

And Growing Spiritually as Partners Does Not Mean . . .

We will discover a mystical and emotional reality.

We will never hurt each other again.

We will only need the Bible and each other.

We will fit someone else's definition of a Christian couple.

We will always feel close and intimate with God and each other.

Heart *2* Heart

When has your faith been tested?

What would you say were the character building times in your life?

What has suffering taught you about living?

What are some good things that have come out of that process?

Only as we love Jesus more than we love each other
are we able to become channels of
God's love.

There is something far more important in our marital relationships than
pleasing each other or making each other happy.

We are to put Christ first in our individual lives, so together we will love
the Lord and become his channel to those in our lives.

Ask yourselves this question.

How are we doing in expressing (through words and actions) our faith as a living reality in front of our friends?

How we relate to each other affects our relationship with God.
How we relate to God affects our marriage.

I commit to making my spiritual relationship my highest priority.

My Tenth Commitment:

Sexuality

Commit to sexuality in your marriage.

When we commit ourselves to sexuality,
we leave behind monotony.

Connecting sexually is the best way to ensure a strong emotional and spiritual bond with your partner.

Learning how to be lovers is a big deal. It's much more than just a physical act. It's about connection, intimacy, closeness, and affection.

It's about being male and female and about becoming one.

But when sex is used destructively in a marriage, it is both the consequence of and the creation of a spiritual problem, a void within us and our relationship.

When sexuality is a healthy, natural part of an intimate connection, it is a key part of the whole relationship.

God wants you to enjoy sex in your marriage. It is a gift created by the same tender Savior who loved each of us enough to give us the ultimate gift of himself.

But just as it is not normal to feel in love with your partner constantly, it is also not normal to feel sexually attracted to him or her all the time.

Circle the words that describe how you perceive sex.

Life-affirming celebration

Emotional isolation

Caring

Open communication

Betrayal of trust

Coercion and fear

Impulsive, compulsive

Disintegration of relationship

Dishonesty and shame

Mutual respect

Enhanced self-esteem

Limited options

Imbalance of power

Emotional intimacy

Dislike of partner

Consent

Heart 2 Heart

Complete the following sentences and discuss with your partner.

The best thing about our sex life is …

My mother and father left me with this impression of sex …

Prior to our marriage I felt sex was …

I find you sexually attractive when …

I find it difficult to initiate sex when …

When I initiate sex, I feel …

A sexual fear I have is …

When I initiate intimacy and you ignore it, I feel …

Does your marriage suffer from sexual difficulties?

Consider and discuss these causes, and don't hesitate to seek a doctor's help.

Family background—(It's something you do because he needs it.)

Cultural attitudes about sex that cause you to feel bad about yourself.

Distorted religious beliefs.

Experiences of physical, emotional, or sexual abuse.

Control issues.

Previous experiences that haunt your bedroom.

Lack of sexual knowledge.

Other _____

YOUR INTIMATE RELATIONSHIP:
Taking Stock

Let these statements be a starting place in your commitment to marital sexuality.

I am intentionally romantic.
I am passionately aware.
I enjoy my own body.
I risk emotional intimacy.
I value change.
I am a skilled lover and talk about our sexual relationship.

I commit to sexuality in our marriage.

My Eleventh Commitment:

Balance

Commit to balance in your marriage.

When we commit ourselves to balance, we leave behind instability.

How often do you go through the day feeling tilted to one side? You're busy all day long but strangely unsatisfied. Are you living off-center?

What is at the center of your life?

When we take care of what is at our center and live out of our center, life takes on purpose, our pursuits are fulfilling, and we feel a deep sense of significance.

We are anchored, as it were, in our soul.

A life without stress would be dull and stagnant.

A life with too much stress is overwhelming, depressing, and dangerous.

Up to a point, stress helps us think, cope, and work better.
Past that point, stress tears us up.

It's essential to find a place of equilibrium where
we have stress without distress.

Periodically every couple needs to ask this question:

Is our life polluting our marriage?

Life is polluting your marriage if at the end of the day ...

you have nothing left for each other.

impatience and anger are your primary emotions.

everything about your partner starts to irritate you.

you find yourself avoiding your partner.

you don't want to help your partner in any practical way.

life is all about you.

It isn't until we come to terms with the fact that time is limited—and that we just have to make choices—that we really consider how we will spend our time.

Heart 2 Heart

Write down the top five priorities that need your focus for the next six months.

What personal values do each of these priorities represent?

In order for those priorities to be important, other things may need to be put aside.

What then will you have to let go of or give very little attention to?

What is one action you can take each day or each week that could move you toward your priority?

An important part of balance is to know when to stop struggling. Leaving your desk for a moment may be an investment in the quality of your life!

Once upon a time, the two of you couldn't wait to be together.

Work was what you did in between being together.

What can you do to reverse this trend?

When you direct your thoughts toward balance, face those things in your life that keep you in a state of instability as if they were an enemy to you and your partner's happiness.

Make a list of things, which if eliminated from your life, would instantly give you a sense of relief.

WHAT RENEWS AND BALANCES YOU—
Taking Stock

Do I build peace and stillness into my life?

When was the last time I set my mind free to be curious,
to be amazed, to enjoy?

Do I give myself permission to rest and accomplish nothing?

Do I take time to pray and meditate?

Keep a gratitude journal.

Before you go to bed, record the blessings of the day.

I commit to balance in our marriage.

My Twelfth Commitment:

Legacy

Commit to legacy in your marriage.

When we commit ourselves to legacy, we
leave behind passivity.

Who are you?
Where are you going?
Why are you going there?

You were created for your life to have meaning and purpose.

When you embrace the dream God has planted inside you, when you discover your destiny, and when you watch God relate his intentions through your life and in your marriage, you will feel incredibly alive.

When we live with a daily awareness of the influence we are exerting and the legacy we are leaving, our every action and word takes on new meaning.

God uses us to carry on his creative work in the lives of the people we touch. We make a difference!

Many of us desire to lead a life of meaning and contribution, but we don't know where to begin.

We are most lost as human beings when we lose connection to our principles, beliefs, and values. On the journey to discover our purpose, we need to ask ourselves:

What do I really enjoy doing?

What energizes and excites me?

What gives my life meaning?

Purpose always serves. It always makes a difference.

In order to live on purpose, focus your energy and effort in the direction of your purpose, whether on or off the job.

Jesus was a follower first and a leader second.

He followed God the Father with all his heart, soul, and mind.

Jesus sought God's will. He submitted to it.

As a result when Christ led, he led with integrity.

What about you?

Do you have someone in your life who will tell you the truth, who will keep you grounded, and who helps keep things in perspective?

Does anyone *really* know you?

Community is the context for character development.

Frustrations in life come from sowing one kind of seed and expecting to reap another.

We must commit time and effort to develop truth in our innermost being.

We often ask: *What are you going to be when you grow up?*

A better question might be: *Who are you going to be when you grow up?*

Notice life's ups and downs.

Enjoy the successes and learn from the failures.

Don't identify with either. They are both temporary.

To live on purpose, we don't have to be independently wealthy,
we don't have to quit our day jobs, and we don't have to
give away all our material possessions.

What we must do is focus our energy and efforts
in the direction of our purpose.

As a couple, you can inspire one another's purpose. By so doing, you build legacy.

Distanced couples look in opposite directions.

Enmeshed couples lose themselves in each other's eyes.

Purposeful couples look outward in the same direction.

What that means is that they are both committed to encouraging and facilitating each other to be all they can be.

Heart 2 Heart

Is there something special that you're meant to contribute to the world?

How does your partner support your quest for purpose?

What does this mean to you personally?

WHAT WILL YOUR FUTURE BE?
Taking Stock

What do you want to accomplish in the next ten years?

What do you most want to learn? Make a list.

What skills do you want to develop? Make a list.

Who would you most like to meet? Where would you most like to go?

Complete this sentence: I feel most energetic and alive when I …

What have you always wanted to do but never allowed yourself to do because it was too expensive, too reckless, or would be too complicated?

On a weekly basis we need to take a "Search Me, O God" personal evaluation. Do this as a gift to those you love.

___ Have I honored my commitments?

___ Have I expressed words of affirmation?

___ Have I demonstrated kindness through my actions and in my attitudes?

___ Have I expressed gratitude through word or deed?

___ Have I talked to and about others respectfully and politely?

___ Have I been generous in my spirit and in my actions?

___ Have I rejoiced with those who rejoice?

Continued

___ Have I wept with those who weep?

___ Have I demonstrated empathy and compassion?

___ Have I done a quiet act of service that wasn't required of me?

___ Have I listened to understand in a conflictive situation?

___ Have I asked someone to forgive me if needed?

___ Have I offered forgiveness to someone?

___ Have I spoken my truth in love?

Continued

___ Have I trusted someone else?

___ Have I been a person of my word?

___ Have I brought joy to those in my sphere of influence?

___ Have I worshipped and fellowshipped with God?

___ Have I submitted to sound counsel?

___ Have I demonstrated loyalty?

Continued

___ Have I made someone laugh?

___ Have I left my world a little better than I found it?

___ Have I demonstrated courage by sticking with my convictions?

___ Have I exercised self-discipline in my words and actions?

___ Have I taken initiative and been proactive?

___ Have I kept eternity forefront in my mind?

We create a legacy one day at a time, one moment at a time.
Ask yourselves:

How do I show up for life?

What is it like to be married to me?

What is it like to be my child?

What is it like to be my friend?

I commit myself to legacy in our marriage.

If we want to be happy together, we need to remember that feelings of love flow from consistent acts of love.

The million-dollar question is:
How can we increase the number of positive moments that we share?

Add these random acts to make your marriage happy!

Write a love letter or poem to your partner.

Create your own list of "Top Ten Reasons Why I Love You."

Create a calendar for one month of the year. Put a surprise on the calendar.
(Examples: I will make your favorite dessert. I want to take you to a
movie of your choice. Enjoy a sensuous massage.)

Create a gratitude journal.

Give your partner a gift of your time and energy.

Commit to practicing your love for your partner and you will be ...
So Happy Together!

About Dr. David and Janet Congo

Dr. David and Janet Congo are founders and directors of LifeMates Ministries, an International Marriage Ministry. David is a licensed clinical psychologist and ordained minister. Janet is a licensed marriage and family therapist and former university instructor. For a number of years they have directed the marriage ministry at Saddleback Church in Lake Forest, California. They have been married for thirty years and have two adult children.

So Happy Together is based on the Congos' book *One Good Year of Marriage*. To get more ideas for improving the quality of your marriage, ask for *One Good Year of Marriage* (ISBN: 0-78143-819-5) at your favorite bookstore.

Additional copies of this book
and other titles from Honor Books are available
wherever good books are sold.

If you have enjoyed this book or it has had
an impact your life, we would like to hear from you.

Please contact us at:

Honor Books
4050 Lee Vance View, Dept. 201
Colorado Springs, CO 80918
Or visit our Web site: www.cookministries.org